The Strange Case of Dr Jekyll and Mr Hyde

A Graphic Revision Guide for GCSE English Literature

Elizabeth May

Brilliant
PUBLICATIONS

We hope you and your pupils enjoy using the ideas in this book. Brilliant Publications publishes many other books to help teachers. To find out more details on any of the titles listed below, please log on to our website: www.brilliantpublications.co.uk.

By the same author
Jane Eyre: A Graphic Revision Guide for GCSE English Literature

Other titles

Published by Brilliant Publications Limited
Unit 10
Sparrow Hall Farm
Edlesborough
Dunstable
Bedfordshire
LU6 2ES, UK

www.brilliantpublications.co.uk

The name Brilliant Publications and the logo are registered trademarks.

Written and illustrated by Elizabeth May
Cover design by Brilliant Publications Limited

© Text and illustrations Elizabeth May 2017
© Design Brilliant Publications Limited 2017

Print   ISBN 978-1-78317-276-4
ePDF   ISBN 978-1-78317-277-1

First printed and published in the UK in 2017

Contents

Introduction

In GCSE English Literature there are long and complicated plots to follow and concepts to grasp that can be overwhelming for any student, and for SEN students in particular, the importance of visuals to aid learning can never be underestimated. 65 per cent of us are visual learners, and all of us can benefit from having large amounts of complex information repackaged in a fun, engaging, and simple way.

This book contains resources that will strengthen students' understanding of Dr Jekyll and Mr Hyde in a format that is easily accessible and highly visual. It serves as a handy revision template to those studying the novella, and serves to be a useful bank of resources for English teachers too. The resources in this book are ideal for photocopying and expanding to larger sizes for students to add notes to, doodle over and colour-code, or equally as part of a structured class activity.

In this book you will find the story of Dr Jekyll and Mr Hyde re-told in comic form, guide pages to aspects of the story, and plenty of activity pages. These resources are all specifically tailored to strengthen the student's understanding of plot, characters, quotes, themes and more; and through using them, learning and revising this iconic novella will become an easier and more fun experience for the student.

How will this book be effective?

Exam specifications

The major exam boards (AQA, Edexcel and OCR) all look for very similar things in order to judge a student's performance. Here are the key skills a student should accomplish in order to score highly. Alongside are the pages in the book relevant to that skill:

Skill	Pages
Understand and analyse words, phrases and sentences in context.	28–33, 41–42
Explore plot, characterisation, settings and events.	6–15, 19–24, 32–34, 37, 41–47
Talk about different themes.	25–31
Generate opinions on the text.	41–44
Support their point of view using quotes and knowledge about context.	16–18, 38–40, 48
Show how language, form and structure of the text shapes its meaning.	6–15, 38–40, 48

SEN

These resources are suitable for any level of study, but are specifically tailored to GCSE study. They are designed to be accessible to students with special educational needs (SEN). To do this, the book uses the following criteria:

* A heavy focus on visuals: using visual aids to learn is an educational recommendation for the vast majority of SEN students. It helps students to remember, understand, get interested in and create associations to the text;
* Simple language for greater accessibility;
* A focus on vocabulary – explaining and rephrasing tricky words;
* A focus on plot comprehension – one of the biggest unaddressed stumbling blocks for SEN students; Chapter summaries are condensed to include key events, and are image-based to help students remember what happened and consolidate a full picture of the plot;
* A focus on key quotes that all students are more likely to comprehend.

Although the book has been created in order to be accessible for SEN students generally, here is how the book can benefit some different types of SEN specifically:

* Provides a large amount of visual aids (LDD, ASD, SLCN, PNI, ADD, Dyslexia);
* Uses clear language (ASD, SLCN);
* Uses vocabulary lists and aims to develop vocabulary (LDD, ASD, SLCN);
* Breaks things down into small steps – particularly plot (LDD, ASD, ADD);
* Uses a range of activities (LDD, ADD);
* Encourages forming an opinion on, and empathising with, characters (ASD, SLCN);
* Repeats specific images and quotes (SLCN, ASD, Dyslexia).

Key:
ADD – Attention Deficit Disorder
ASD – Autistic Spectrum Disorder
LDD – Learning Difficulties and Disabilities
PNI – Physical and Neurological Impairments
SLCN – Speech, Language and Communication Needs

1 STORY OF THE DOOR

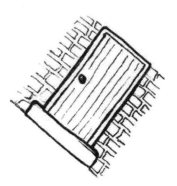

Utterson

Enfield

Here is Mr Utterson, a respectable lawyer, and his friend, Mr Enfield.

I've got a crazy story about that place.

They are taking their Sunday walk around London, when Enfield spots a building he recognises.

Aaeagh!

In Enfield's story, a hideous man trampled over a girl.

An angry mob surrounded the man.

The hideous man told the mob he would make amends.

He went inside a nearby building …

£100

and came back with a cheque for £100, bribing the mob not to say anything.

The strange thing is …

That cheque was signed by a good, reputable man.

Could this good man have been blackmailed?

The strange man's name was …

Hyde?!

– and Utterson has heard of him.

2 SEARCH FOR MR. HYDE

I bet the man's name on that cheque was **Jekyll** ...

Utterson sorts through a load of documents until ...

… HE FINDS JEKYLL'S WILL!

"I leave everything to Mr Hyde."

WHAT??

Utterson goes to see his friend Dr Lanyon to ask him about Jekyll.

Dr. Lanyon

Jekyll? He used to be a good friend.

But not anymore, since our big argument.

Never heard of Hyde.

Jekyll

Utterson keeps wondering how Jekyll and Hyde could be involved with each other.

Hyde

He decides he will try to catch Hyde.

MONDAY

Utterson

TUESDAY

Utterson

WEDNESDAY

Utterson

FINALLY!

Aha!

Hyde

Wow, he's hideous!

Utterson has the feeling that Hyde is so evil that Jekyll has to be warned. He goes to Jekyll's house but he isn't in. Instead he chats to Jekyll's butler, Poole, who reveals …

Poole

Oh no!

Jekyll said I have to obey Hyde as well as him. Everyone working for Jekyll has to obey him.

What if Hyde plans to kill Jekyll to get his money?

3 DR JEKYLL WAS QUITE AT EASE

Two weeks later, Jekyll throws a nice dinner party.

Utterson

Jekyll

Bye!

Utterson stayed behind after everyone left.

Jekyll, I think you should be worried!

He tells all his worries to Jekyll.

You sound as crazy as Lanyon.

But Jekyll just laughs it off.

Then Jekyll gets serious.

Stop asking about my will, Utterson!

I have taken an interest in Mr Hyde ...

and I want you, as my lawyer, to make sure my will is carried out.

4 THE CAREW MURDER CASE 1 year later...

A maid sees Hyde killing an old man, Carew, with a cane.

She calls the police and tells them about the murder.

The police come, and they find a letter for Utterson on Carew's body.

The police call Utterson and he comes along. He sees the broken cane and recognises it…

He gave it to Jekyll years ago!

Utterson, the murderer was a man called Hyde.

What? Hyde? Let's go to his house!

KNOCK KNOCK

Hyde's evil-looking landlady

Come in then...

Utterson and the police look around the house. It is messy – like Hyde left in a rush.

clothes everywhere

drawers pulled out

half a cane

I found the other half of the murder weapon!

And I found half of a cheque book!

5 INCIDENT OF THE LETTER

Utterson is worried. He goes to visit Jekyll.

Poole

Yes, follow me.

Is Jekyll in?

LABORATORY

So he's in here?

Yes.

Jekyll looks "deadly sick".

Tremble Shiver

Jekyll did you hear about what happened to Carew?

Yes, I heard about Carew's murder...

and I want you to know that I will never see Hyde again.

Look at the note he left me ...

Dear Jekyll,
Don't worry about me. I've escaped. Thank you for being so generous.
from Hyde

Utterson asks an important question.

Jekyll, did Hyde **force** you to leave him all your money in your will?

YES!

I knew it! He plans to kill you!

On the way out ...

Poole, who came to hand that note to Jekyll?

What do you mean? Nobody came to hand in a note.

That evening ...

How strange.

Mr Guest, my friend! Come over!

Utterson has an idea – his friend Mr Guest can help him compare Jekyll's handwriting to the handwriting on Hyde's note.

Utterson, the writing is almost the exact same

Mr Guest

Oh no! Is Jekyll trying to **help** a **murderer**?

Hyde has gone missing …

and Jekyll is happier and healthier.

Jekyll

Utterson

I'm so glad Hyde has left Jekyll alone!

But one day …

Poole

Sorry, Jekyll won't see anyone.

For the whole week, Jekyll would not see anyone.

Still no.

I need to ask Lanyon if he knows anything about this.

Hello, Lanyon. Oh … oh dear, what happened to you?

Utterson, I will die. I have had a shock and I'll never recover.

Jekyll is ill too.

Lanyon looks sick and frightened.

I don't want to talk about Jekyll!

Utterson wonders what is going on and writes a letter to Jekyll.

Dear Jekyll, What's all this with Lanyon? Love, Utterson

Jekyll writes back…

I don't want to see Lanyon! I want to be left alone!

Two weeks later, Lanyon dies.

He leaves a letter for Utterson.

The envelope says:

PRIVATE: Only for Utterson to read.

Do not open until the death of Jekyll.

Utterson wants to open it now, but resists.

Utterson also stops trying to see Jekyll.

 # INCIDENT AT THE WINDOW

Utterson and Enfield take their usual Sunday walk.

"Hey look, it's that door again!"

"I found out that this building is connected to Jekyll's house!"

"Hey, look! That's Jekyll in the window!"

"I am very low, Utterson."

"I hope you are okay, Jekyll."

"You stay in too much. Walk with us!"

"I want to ... but I can't."

Suddenly, Jekyll freezes ...

and looks **terrified**.

Utterson and Enfield walk away, shocked by Jekyll's terrified expression.

SLAM

"Oh dear!"

"God forgive us."

9 DR LANYON'S NARRATIVE

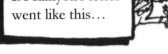
Dr Lanyon's letter went like this…

I received a letter from Jekyll.

Lanyon, please do me a favour! Find my powder, phial and paper book.

Can you take those 3 things to my lab at midnight? Someone will be there to collect them. — Jekyll

---

I did what Jekyll asked and took the 3 things to his lab.

At midnight, Mr Hyde showed up!

Have you got it? Have you got it?

Yes … just here.

Ah!

Mr Hyde mixed some chemicals together to make a potion.

He drank the potion.

His face became suddenly black.

His features started to change.

And in front of me stood Jekyll!

I am so scared and disturbed by what I have seen. I can't even sleep. I must die.

Lanyon

This is what Jekyll's letter said.

I was always a good, respectable, wealthy man.

But I always wondered about man's dual nature – the good and bad side of everyone.

I did experiments that let me turn into Hyde and live on the bad side.

It felt great to be bad.

But soon, things got out of control . . . . I killed Carew, the politician.

Then I started to transform into Hyde without the potion!

Oh no.

Hyde became stronger, and I became weaker.

I tried making the potion again. I slipped notes under the door asking Poole to find ingredients for the potion.

But nothing worked.

I have run out of time. I bring the life of that unhappy Jekyll to an end.

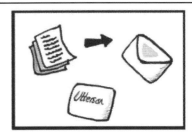

Jekyll finishes writing this letter just before Utterson and Poole come. He leaves it for Utterson to find.

Context

> **Context** means the situation, or circumstances something is in. If we know about the context of a book, it helps us to understand why it was written and how people reading it would have reacted at the time.

Victorian London

Time: 19th century (1800s). The Victorian times were between 1837–1901. Stevenson wrote the story in 1885 and set it around the same time.

Place: London, England. At the time, London held more people than any other city in the world.

The 19th century was a time when **science** and **technology** grew fast, when the Victorians discovered that people had **evolved** from primates. A lot of them wondered if they could still **believe in God**. Some people thought scientists should not do experiments and discover new things, because it was like pretending to be God. Furthermore, Victorians were very **repressed**, which means they were under a lot of pressure to appear **good** and **reputable**. Because of this, no one really knew what **secrets** people were hiding.

Robert Louis Stevenson

Robert Louis Stevenson was born in 1850 in Scotland. When he was young, he **travelled a lot,** but was also often very ill. As he became an adult, he became interested in the 'dark side' of Edinburgh, and started to question whether or not he should believe in God. Stevenson wrote a lot of his stories in the 1880s, when he was in his 30s.

He wrote Dr Jekyll and Mr Hyde very **quickly** – it only took him a few days. He had the idea for the book after having a **nightmare** about changing into a monster. The book was **short** and **cheap** to buy when it was released. It was very **popular**; it sold a huge amount of copies and helped Stevenson become a **famous** author.

Gothic Fiction

Gothic fiction is a style of novel that was popular during the 18th and 19th centuries. These novels usually involved dark, sometimes scary themes.

Gothic fiction might include any of the following:

✳ Supernatural elements (such as ghosts, vampires, monsters)

✳ Religion (usually Christianity)

✳ A mystery

✳ Loneliness

✳ A villain (an evil character)

✳ Romance

✳ Strong emotions (people overreacting or being extremely sad, extremely happy, and so on)

Gothic Fiction

Some people think that Dr Jekyll and Mr Hyde is a Gothic novel because it was written at the time when Gothic fiction was popular and because the story involves some of the key Gothic themes. It is up to you to decide whether you think it is a Gothic novel or not. Fill out the table below to help you decide.

Gothic theme	Is it a part of the story? If yes, when?
Supernatural elements	
Religion	
A mystery	
Loneliness	
A villain	
Romance	
Strong emotions	

JEKYLL

Full name: Dr Henry Jekyll

Also known as: *Harry, "the doctor"*

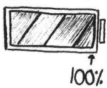

IMPORTANCE:

100%

Fact file:

* Jekyll is popular and sociable.

* He comes from a rich, reputable family.

* When he was younger he did bad things that he kept secret.

* He thinks everyone has two sides: a good side and an evil side.

* He makes a potion that turns him into his evil side: Hyde.

> Man is not truly one, but truly two.

Appearance:

Jekyll is a "large, well-made, smooth-faced man of fifty." This means Jekyll is **tall** and looks **healthy**. Although he is fifty, he still **looks young**.

What people say about him:

ENFIELD

> The very pink of the proprieties, and celebrated too, and ... one of your fellows who do what they call **good**.

chapter 1

> An **honest** man

chapter 1

chapter 2

> Henry Jekyll became too **fanciful** for me.

LANYON

> He began to go wrong, **wrong** in mind.

chapter 2

POOLE

chapter 8

> A **tall**, **fine** build of a man.

chapter 3

> (Jekyll has) something of a **slyish** cast perhaps, but every mark of capacity and **kindness**.

STEVENSON (author and narrator)

HYDE

Full name: Mr Edward Hyde
Also known as: *"the creature"*

Fact file:

✳ Hyde is Jekyll after he takes a potion to transform his body.

✳ Being Hyde, Jekyll lets his 'evil side' out and does all the bad things he wants to do.

✳ Hyde is younger than Jekyll, is lower class, and does not have the same good reputation as him.

IMPORTANCE:

100%

What do you want?

Appearance

Hyde is a very **small** man. He is **skinny** and **hairy**. His face is **strange** and **scary**. He looks almost like he **isn't human**. He is described as "'wicked-looking", "pale and dwarfish" and "revolting".

What people say about him:

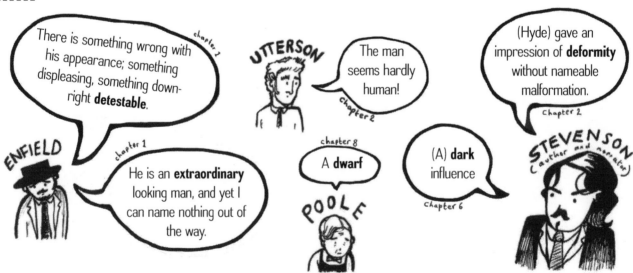

There is something wrong with his appearance; something displeasing, something down-right **detestable**. — *chapter 1*

UTTERSON

The man seems hardly human! — *chapter 2*

(Hyde) gave an impression of **deformity** without nameable malformation. — *chapter 2*

ENFIELD

He is an **extraordinary** looking man, and yet I can name nothing out of the way. — *chapter 1*

A **dwarf** — *chapter 8*

POOLE

(A) **dark** influence — *chapter 6*

STEVENSON (author and narrator)

UTTERSON

Full name: Mr Gabriel John Utterson

Also known as: "the lawyer"

IMPORTANCE:

↑ 100%

Fact file:

❋ Utterson is a sensible, professional man.

❋ He has a good reputation.

❋ He can be shy and awkward around people, but he cares about his friends a lot.

❋ In the book, he spends a lot of time worrying about Jekyll and being shocked about things he finds out.

I shall be Mr Seek!

Appearance:

Utterson is "a man of rugged countenance that was never lighted by a smile", which means his face looks **rough** and **tired** and he does not smile. He is "lean, long, dusty, dreary and yet **somehow loveable**", so he looks plain and boring, but nice too.

What people say about him:

JEKYLL

chapter 3

I would **trust** (Utterson) before any man alive, ay, before myself, if I could make the choice.

chapter 3

Where Utterson was liked, he was **liked well**.

chapter 1

(He was) inclined to **help** rather than reprove.

STEVENSON (author and narrator)

LANYON

Full name: Dr Hastie Lanyon

IMPORTANCE:

75%

Fact file:

✳ Lanyon is a scientist like Jekyll.

✳ He stopped talking to Jekyll after they had a big argument about science.

✳ He likes the traditional, rational, logical type of science – not the strange experiments Jekyll does.

✳ He dies after seeing Hyde transform into Jekyll.

My life is shaken to the roots ...

Appearance:

Lanyon is "a hearty, healthy, dapper, red-faced gentleman, with a shock of hair prematurely white". This means Lanyon looks **healthy** (although maybe a bit fat). "Dapper" means he is **well dressed**. His **hair has turned white** even though he is too young for that to happen.

What people say about him:

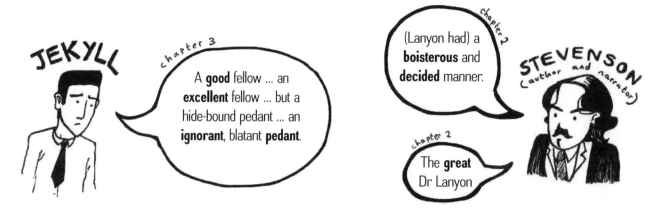

JEKYLL

chapter 3

A **good** fellow ... an **excellent** fellow ... but a hide-bound pedant ... an **ignorant**, blatant **pedant**.

chapter 2

(Lanyon had) a **boisterous** and **decided** manner.

STEVENSON (author and narrator)

chapter 2

The **great** Dr Lanyon

ENFIELD

Full name: Mr Richard Enfield

Fact file:

* Enfield is Utterson's cousin.

* He is good friends with Utterson, even though they are different – Enfield is talkative, sociable and always out doing something.

* He always goes for a walk with Utterson on Sunday evening.

* He has a strong sense of right and wrong.

* He sees Hyde trample the girl in Chapter 1, but did not want to tell Utterson that Hyde had a link to Jekyll.

IMPORTANCE: 60%

Did you ever remark that door?

What people say about him:

STEVENSON (author and narrator)

chapter 1

The well-known man about town

The Strange Case of Dr Jekyll and Mr Hyde: A Graphic Revision Guide

OTHER CHARACTERS

POOLE

Also known as: "the servant'

Appearance: "a well-dressed elderly servant"

* Poole works at Jekyll's house as his butler. This means he is in charge of the house and all the other staff there.

* He has been Jekyll's butler for 20 years.

* He is polite, kind and very worried about his master.

CAREW

Full name: Sir Danvers Carew

Appearance: "an aged and beautiful gentleman with white hair"

* Carew is a Member of Parliament (MP), so a lot of people know and like him.

* Utterson is his lawyer.

* He is murdered by Hyde in Chapter 4.

GUEST

Also known as: "the clerk"

* Guest is a friend of Utterson's from work.
* Utterson trusts him and shares his secrets with him.
* Guest is an expert in analysing handwriting, and helps Utterson compare Jekyll and Hyde's handwriting in Chapter 5.

BRADSHAW

Also known as: "the footman"

* Bradshaw is another member of staff at Jekyll's house.

* Poole is his boss.

* He appears in Chapter 8, and is scared about what has happened to Jekyll.

* He is described as "very white and nervous".

What is a Theme?

A theme is an idea that comes up again and again. The author will put themes in a book because they want the reader to think about certain things.

Themes carry messages and help to create an effect on the reader.

Here are some of the themes in Dr Jekyll and Mr Hyde:

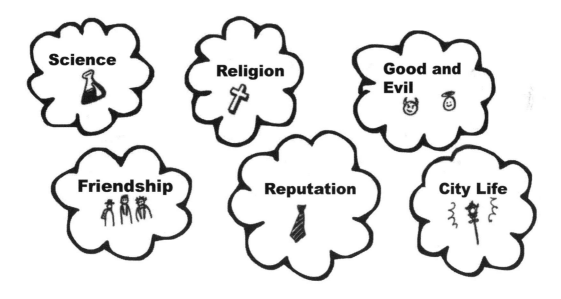

Use the following pages to help you decide which of these are linked to each other.

Remember – you can talk about themes in any exam question.

THEME: Reputation

In Victorian times, it was very important to be well respected and to look as if you were a good, noble person. This is called having a good reputation. If you have a good reputation, a lot of people know who you are and think nice things about you.

Quotes about reputation:

chapter 1

ENFIELD

The person that drew that cheque is the very pink of the proprieties, celebrated too, and (what makes it worse), one of your fellows who do what they call good.

chapter 1

(Utterson) was austere with himself; drank gin when he was alone, to mortify a taste for vintages; and though he enjoyed the theatre, had not crossed the doors of one for twenty years.

chapter 5

JEKYLL

I cannot say I care what becomes of Hyde: I am quite done with him. I was thinking of my own character, which this hateful business has rather exposed.

chapter 3

(Jekyll) gave one of his pleasant dinners to some five or six old cronies, all intelligent and reputable men.

STEVENSON
(author and narrator)

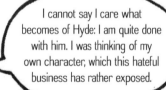

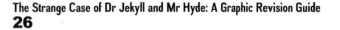

THEME: Science

Since two important characters in the books are scientists (Jekyll and Lanyon), science is a big part of the story. Without the theme of science, there would be no story – Jekyll has to be a scientist so he can make the potion that turns him into Hyde.

Lanyon's Science

Lanyon likes traditional, old-fashioned, normal science – the way it has always been done. He thinks Jekyll's experiments are "wrong" and "unscientific".

Jekyll's Science

Jekyll's type of science is called "transcendental medicine". Jekyll experiments with chemicals and makes the potion that turns him into Hyde.

Quotes about science:

UTTERSON — chapter 2
(Jekyll and Lanyon) have only differed on some point of science ... it is nothing worse than that.

LANYON — chapter 6
I sometimes think that if we knew all, we should be more glad to get away.

JEKYLL — chapter 10
I compounded the elements, watched them boil and smoke together in the glass, and ... drank off the potion.

THEME:
Good and Evil

Jekyll believes that every person has a good side and an evil side. He thinks people show their good side but keep their evil side hidden. This is an idea that relates to the context of the book, because in Victorian England, it was important to look like a good person, even if you were not.

Quotes about good and evil:

chapter 10

I had now two characters as well as two appearances, one was wholly evil, and the other was still the old Henry Jekyll.

JEKYLL

chapter 10

I knew myself, at the first breath of this new life, to be more wicked, tenfold more wicked.

chapter 10

It was on the moral side, and in my own person, that I learned to recognise the thorough and primitive duality of man.

chapter 4

An ivory-faced and silvery-haired old woman opened the door. She had an evil face, smooth by hypocrisy: but her manners were excellent.

chapter 1

It was frequently (Utterson's) fortune to be the last reputable acquaintance and the last good influence in the lives of downgoing men.

STEVENSON

THEME: Religion

In the 1800s, people were much more religious than they are in England today. Most people would have been Christians, so it is likely that the characters in the story are Christians.

On the other hand, in the 1800s people got quite confused about religion. This is because there were new scientific discoveries, so people learned more about how the world worked. For example, people learned about how humans evolved from primates. Christians began to wonder if what they believed was really true.

Stevenson might have used religion as a theme in the story because:

✳ It helps to show the difference between the past, where Christians could believe in their religion without being challenged, and the present, when religion was questioned.

✳ It helps to show characters as either good or bad.

Quotes about religion:

UTTERSON

chapter 1
I incline to Cain's heresy ... I let my brother go to the devil in his own way.

chapter 7
God forgive us, God forgive us

Chapter 8
Amen, Poole.

POOLE

chapter 8
We heard him cry out in the name of God ... a thing that cries to Heaven.

chapter 8
God grant there be nothing wrong.

THEME:
City Life

London in the 1800s was bigger than it had ever been and was still growing very fast. Too many people were in London, so a lot of people had to live in 'slums', which were very small, unclean, overcrowded houses. All kinds of people lived close together and a lot of crime happened.

In the book, Stevenson describes London as a mysterious place. The streets are often dark, foggy and windy, and characters feel scared walking around.

Quotes about city life:

chapter 1
The street shone out in contrast to its dingy neighbourhood.

STEVENSON
(author and narrator)

chapter 8
Mr Utterson thought he had never seen that part of London so deserted.

chapter 4
London was startled by a crime of singular ferocity.

chapter 8
London hummed solemnly all around.

THEME: Friendship

Without his friends, Utterson would never have been able to piece together the mystery of Jekyll and Hyde. He would also not have anyone to tell his secrets and worries to. Even though Utterson is awkward and not great at conversations, friendship is one of the most important parts of his life.

It is important that Lanyon and Jekyll's argument is about something that eventually kills both of them. Could Stevenson be telling us that friendship should be very important to all of us?

Quotes about friendship:

(Utterson) had an approved tolerance for others.

chapter 1

Mr Hyde had numbered few familiars.

chapter 4

JEKYLL

chapter 3

My good Utterson ... I would trust you before any man alive.

(Utterson and Lanyon) were old friends ... men who thoroughly enjoyed each other's company.

chapter 2

STEVENSON

(author & narrator)

Jekyll's Laboratory
('Blackmail House')

"The doors from one corner, on the left hand going east, the line was broken by the entry of a court; and just at that point, a certain sinister block of building thrust forward its gable on the street. It was **two stories high**; showed **no window, nothing but a door on the lower storey** and a blind forehead of **discoloured wall** on the upper; and bore in every feature the marks of prolonged and sordid **negligence**."

INSIDE Jekyll's Laboratory

"It was a **large** room, fitted round with **glass presses**, furnished, among other things, with a **cheval-glass** and a **business table** and looking out upon the court by **three dusty windows barred with iron**."

Hyde's house

"In the whole extent of the house, which but for the old woman remained otherwise **empty**, Mr Hyde had only used a couple of rooms; but these were furnished with **luxury** and good taste. A closet was **filled** with wine; the plate was of **silver**, the napery **elegant**; a **good picture** hung upon the walls, a gift (as Utterson supposed) from Henry Jekyll, who was much of a connoisseur; and the carpets were of many plies and **agreeable in colour**. At this moment, however, the rooms bore the mark of being recently and hurriedly **ransacked; clothes lay about the floor**, with their pockets inside-out; lock-fast **drawers stood open**; and on the hearth there lay **a pile of grey ashes,** as though many papers had been burned."

Jekyll's Will

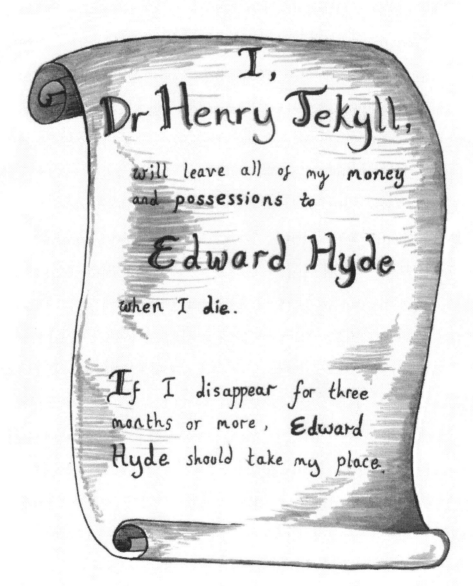

I,
Dr Henry Jekyll,
will leave all of my money and possessions to

Edward Hyde

when I die.

If I disappear for three months or more, Edward Hyde should take my place.

The Strange Case of Dr Jekyll and Mr Hyde: A Graphic Revision Guide

Jekyll's Invitation to dinner, chapter 3

DR. HENRY JEKYLL

invites you to a pleasant

Dinner Party

Where: Dr Henry Jekyll's house
When: 7pm til Late

Expect intelligent company

good wine

and a warm fire!

Carew's Murder in the News

The London News

Buy Daily

October 18—

LONDON'S BEST NEWSPAPER

CAREW MURDERED

M.P. SIR DANVERS CAREW BRUTALLY KILLED

THE CITY IS IN SHOCK as one of London's beloved Members of Parliament, Sir Danvers Carew, was killed last night. The incident happened under the full moon in a central London street, near to the Thames river.

One person witnessed the incident. A maid, who saw the killing through her window, said "I saw Carew come along and admired his beauty, innocence and old-world kindness. A small man approached him and started beating him. It was so horrible that I fainted."

Carew outside his London home.

The maid called the police after she regained consciousness. Police found half of a cane at the scene. Early reports are linking the incident to London resident Mr Edward Hyde, who matches the maid's description and has reportedly been violent before.

Vocabulary

Here are some words that are important in the book and in some of the quotes.

Word	Quote	Meaning
austere	"(Utterson) was **austere** with himself." *(Chapter 1)*	Strict. Not having fun.
Juggernaut	"It wasn't like a man; it was like some damned **Juggernaut**." *(Chapter 1)*	A huge cart carrying a statue of a God. This unstoppable cart crushed a lot of people.
cheque	"(Hyde) came back with the matter of ten pounds in gold and a **cheque** for the balance." *(Chapter 1)*	A piece of paper that tells the bank to pay a certain amount of money.
deformed	"(Hyde) must be **deformed** somewhere." *(Chapter 1)*	Something unusual or strange about the body.
will	"(Utterson) opened his safe, took from the most private part of it a document endorsed on the envelope as Dr Jekyll's **Will**, and sat down with a clouded brow to study its contents." *(Chapter 2)*	A document that a person writes to say who gets to keep their money and property after they die.
fanciful	"It is more than ten years since Henry Jekyll became too **fanciful** for me." *(Chapter 2)*	Getting carried away. Hoping and imagining too much.

Here are some words that are important in the book and in some of the quotes.

Word	Quote	Meaning
balderdash	"Such unscientific **balderdash**" *(Chapter 2)*	Nonsense.
pedant	"O, I know (Lanyon's) a good fellow ... an excellent fellow ... but a hide-bound **pedant** for all that; an ignorant, blatant **pedant**." *(Chapter 3)*	Someone who sticks to the rules and doesn't like new things.
cane	"(Hyde) had in his hand a heavy **cane**." *(Chapter 4)*	A stick with a handle to help you walk.
ransacked	"The rooms bore every mark of having been recently and hurriedly **ransacked**." *(Chapter 4)*	Searched messily.
familiars	"Mr Hyde had numbered few **familiars**." *(Chapter 4)*	Friends or acquaintances.
clerk	"The **clerk** ... was a man of counsel." *(Chapter 5)*	A person who works in an office.
despair	"The smile was struck out of (Jekyll's) face and succeeded by an expression of such abject terror and **despair**, as froze the very blood of the two gentlemen below." *(Chapter 7)*	Hopelessness.

Vocabulary

Here are some words that are important in the book and in some of the quotes.

Word	Quote	Meaning
doubled up	"The creature was so **doubled up**" *(Chapter 8)*	Bent over or curled up.
phial	"By the crushed **phial** in (Hyde's) hand and the strong smell of kernels that hung in the air, Utterson knew that he was looking on the body of a self-destroyer." *(Chapter 8)*	A small glass container that holds liquids.
cheval-glass	"The searchers came to a **cheval-glass** into whose depths they looked with an involuntary horror." *(Chapter 8)*	A full length mirror that can be tilted.
narrative	"Go then, and first read the **narrative** which Lanyon warned me he was to place in your hands." *(Chapter 8)*	A telling of a story (Dr Lanyon's letter to Utterson, in this case).
thorough	"It was on the moral side, and in my own person, that I learned to recognise the **thorough** and **primitive duality** of man." *(Chapter 10)*	Complete.
primitive		Natural; part of what it is to be human.
duality		Being two things at once (eg both good and bad).

Match the quote to the picture

My devil had been long caged, he came out roaring.

We heard him cry out upon the name of God.

She became aware of an aged beautiful gentleman with white hair ... and advancing to meet him, another and very small gentleman.

An ivory-faced and silvery-haired old woman opened the door. She had an evil face, smoothed by hypocrisy: but her manners were excellent.

He began slowly to mount the street, pausing every step or two, and putting his hand to his brow, like a man in mental perplexity.

It was his custom of a Sunday ... to sit close by the fire, a volume of some dry divinity on his reading desk.

Match the quote to the picture

He was dressed in clothes far too large for him, clothes of the doctor's bigness.

It was on the moral side, and in my own person, I learned to recognise the thorough and primitive duality of man.

He was austere with himself (and) drank gin when he was alone.

Here then, as I lay down my pen ... I bring the life of that unhappy Henry Jekyll to an end.

His face became suddenly black and the features seemed to melt and alter.

The rooms bore every mark of having been recently and hurriedly ransacked.

Fill in the missing word

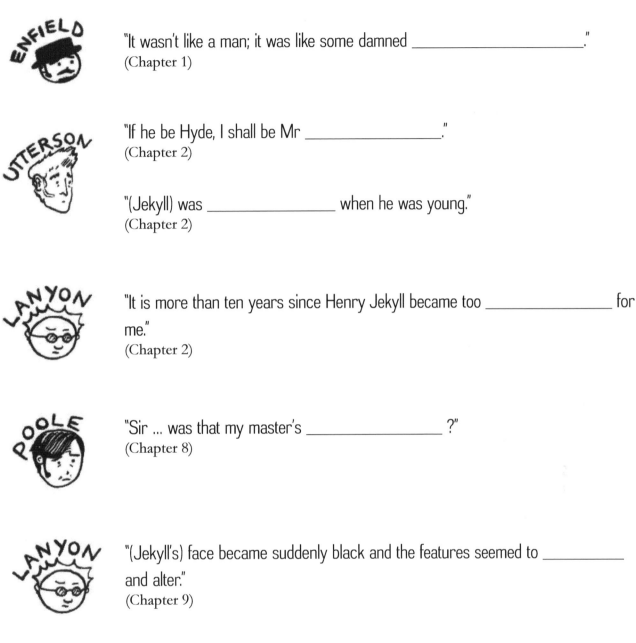

ENFIELD

"It wasn't like a man; it was like some damned _____."
(Chapter 1)

UTTERSON

"If he be Hyde, I shall be Mr _____."
(Chapter 2)

"(Jekyll) was _____ when he was young."
(Chapter 2)

LANYON

"It is more than ten years since Henry Jekyll became too _____ for me."
(Chapter 2)

POOLE

"Sir ... was that my master's _____ ?"
(Chapter 8)

LANYON

"(Jekyll's) face became suddenly black and the features seemed to _____ and alter."
(Chapter 9)

JEKYLL

"I knew myself, at the first breath of this new life, to be more _____, tenfold more _____."
(Chapter 10)

Draw one picture that you think summarises each chapter

STORY OF THE DOOR

1

SEARCH FOR MR HYDE

2

DR JEKYLL WAS QUITE AT EASE

3

THE CAREW MURDER CASE

4

INCIDENT OF THE LETTER

5

REMARKABLE INCIDENT OF DR LANYON

6

INCIDENT AT THE WINDOW

7

THE LAST NIGHT

8

DR LANYON'S NARRATIVE

9

HENRY JEKYLL'S FULL STATEMENT OF THE CASE

10

TOP TRUMPS

Give the characters a mark out of ten for each quality and compare them. You could even cut the cards out and play a quick game of Top Trumps with a classmate.

Henry Jekyll

Honesty . . . .
Friendship . . . .
Curiosity . . . . . .
Evil . . . .

Edward Hyde

Honesty . . . .
Friendship . . . . . .
Curiosity . . . . . .
Evil . . . .

Gabriel Utterson

Honesty . . . .
Friendship . . . .
Curiosity . . . . . .
Evil . . . .

Hastie Lanyon

Honesty . . . .
Friendship . . . .
Curiosity . . . .
Evil . . . .

Richard Enfield

Honesty . . . .
Friendship . . . .
Curiosity . . . .
Evil . . . .

Poole

Honesty . . . .
Friendship . . . . . .
Curiosity . . . . . .
Evil . . . .

Draw Utterson's expression when...

... he returned home after hearing Enfield's story about Hyde (chapter 2).

... Poole tells him that all of Jekyll's staff must obey Hyde too (chapter 2).

... he sees Jekyll in his laboratory and Jekyll tells him Hyde forced him to write the will (chapter 5).

... Guest tells him Jekyll's handwriting is almost the same as Hyde's (chapter 5).

... he and Enfield see Jekyll's terrified expression through the window (chapter 7).

... he breaks into Jekyll's lab and sees Hyde dead on the floor (chapter 8).

How would you feel if...

You found out your friend gave money to an evil criminal?
(happens to Utterson, chapter 1)

Two of your friends become very sick, but neither of them will tell you why?
(happens to Utterson, chapters 5 and 6)

You could do evil things and get away with it?
(happens to Jekyll/Hyde)

The person you worked for for over 20 years suddenly disappears?
(happens to Poole, chapter 8)

You saw a brutal murder happen in the middle of the night?
(happens to the maid, chapter 4)

You discover everything you thought you know about your favourite thing in the world is actually all wrong?
(happens to Lanyon, chapters 6 and 9)

You had to die because of your own mistakes? *(happens to Jekyll, chapter 10)*

Turn Jekyll into Hyde

Below is Jekyll, the tall, healthy, young-looking scientist. With a pencil, draw over him to turn him into his evil side, Hyde. Use the descriptions of Hyde from the story to help you.

Dr Lanyon's
transformation

In Chapter 2, Stevenson describes Lanyon as "a hearty, healthy, dapper, red-faced gentleman". However, in Chapter 6, Lanyon's appearance changes after he has a big shock. Look at the description of Lanyon and draw on the picture below to show how Lanyon changes.

Find an important quote said <u>by</u> this character:

Find an important quote said <u>about</u> this character:

List 5 adjectives to describe them:

They like…

Character:

Age:
_____

They dislike…

Job:
_____

How do they dress?
_____
_____
_____

Draw them here:

How much do I like this character? (circle)

Where do they live?

Draw an item that links to them:

List 3 important things that happen to them in the story:

① _____

② _____

③ _____

Who are their friends?

QUOTE ANALYSIS

Chapter: Page: Said by:

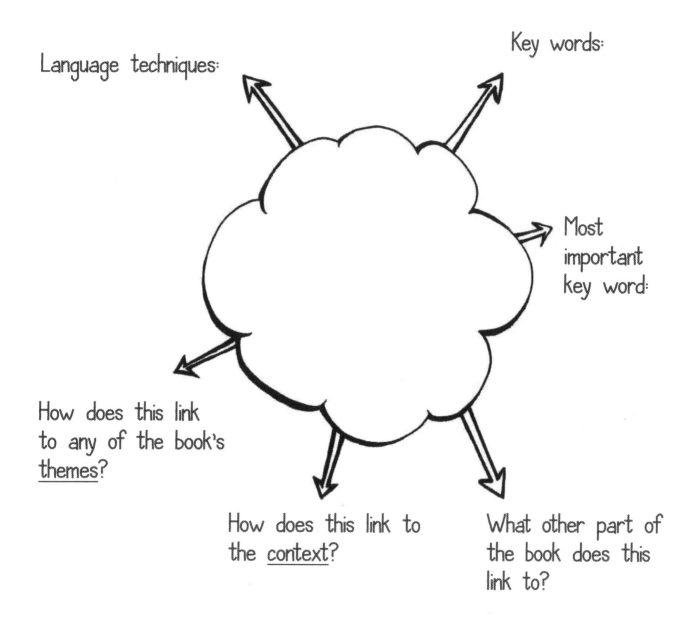

Language techniques:

Key words:

Most
important
key word:

How does this link
to any of the book's
themes?

How does this link to
the context?

What other part of
the book does this
link to?